FOR THE SAKE OF MY SANITY

One Woman's Journey of Speaking Truth to Power and Ignorance

DrLoni

This book is dedicated to:

The wounded little girl inside of me;
may she be healed and know that she is loved.

TABLE OF CONTENTS

Preface vii

End White Silence...1

Sisters Reading Sisters* 21

Grandparent's Love 35

What Am I So Happy About? 41

Why I Don't Date White Men 49

No Salute 59

Fighting Kindness 63

Poverty 67

You Are All of My Joy 73

DrLoni Ain't No Nickname 79

Stars n' Stripes 83

I Can't Believe What Some Folks Don't Even Think About 87

Soft By Nature Hard Without a Choice 93

Skin-tone 97

Weeds..103

The Magic of Forty...107

A Call To Action 113

Final Word..121

PREFACE

If you love my expression of feelings
Please do not trap me into silence
Making me solely responsible for all my inner thoughts

I am the voice of the women who cannot speak
The tear drops of children *that* do not understand for
which they are shed
Any voice trapped into submission

I am there only because you have walked the path
Maybe one day we will meet
Maybe we will not

I will be gentle
Listen
Only try to express what I know you would be able to express better

My feelings are mine
Yours
The world around them
Take credit silent voices... let us speak

Yolanda M. Johnson - circa 1980

If I did not write, I would have died. Period. End of story. But as an offering for meeting me at this place, I will share how my writing was something that I had to do for the sake of my sanity. It provided the platform for me to exorcise the issues of isolation, abandonment and depression, my three very best friends, for most of my life.

This book does not define who I am; it is a release of that which no longer defines me.

Coming to terms with my own power has been a life long process. At the age of forty-five, now forty-eight, I decided that I must put this book together for my own liberation. In many ways I feel it is too late, but I have come to accept that everything in my life is right on time. The feeling that there is something very special about me and that someday I would possess a great deal of power and influence has been with me since I was a little girl. Thus, taking so long to pursue my passions full throttle has been an intentional delay of the enviable; just another iteration of the fear of success. Mind you, currently I do not possess a great deal of power; correction... currently, I am not mindful of how powerful I already am. Writing and publishing this book is my initiation into claiming my voice and power.

This is my first public speaking out about the abuse I have experienced. Writing about these things is an act of self-love because I realized that the way I have lived my life was done on the terms of others to satisfy them and not myself. Publishing this book is about finding the courage to speak about that which has scared and scarred me so that my healing might begin.

As an adult I am responsible for my own suffering, as well as, my own liberation. As a child I chose to ignore the mean words and persistent bad attitude of others, not expressing how badly it made me feel, because I did not feel I had a choice. Quite frankly, as a child, I did not have a choice. Very early in my life I was badly beaten for crying because I was not able to articulate why I was crying. The rest of my childhood was one without tears, not expressing any discontent, or doing anything "wrong" so that in my child's mind, I would not be beaten or come under more attack.

Too often children must find coping mechanisms to deal with the stress or abuse in their lives without any support from sympathetic adults. Many times those who can help them, teachers and other family, are unaware of the disfunction in a child's life, while the children do not yet know that what they are experiencing is unhealthy. Too many adults treat children as if they are immune to the toxicity around them. These adults expose children to unhealthy situations, yet never pause to help them process what has occurred. Children are truly sponges who absorb and internalize all that occurs around them. When they are left to understand the adult world with a child's heart and mind, too often they sadly move into adulthood with a wounded child inside of an adult body. This has been my journey.

Parenting, the act of nurturing the growth of a child and having the unconditional trust of that child, is a sacred bond. If no one is present to do right by a child, dealing lovingly with their spirit, the child's ability to negotiate a better reality for themselves is limited. If you dishonor that trust and injure them without atonement, then you are responsible for causing pain and injury to an innocent victim. The guilt which may inevitable plague adults who injure children does not undue the damage done to the child. The world is left with yet another person in an adult body, sometimes knowingly, often not, dealing with the consequences of an injured spirit.

As a child I felt forced to accept the very clear conditional terms of how some people chose to love me. In my child's head to get others to "act" like they loved me, I did what they wanted me to do so they would "talk nice to me" and I would temporarily win their affection. As an adult, I am the one who pretended to want whatever my abuser wanted, because I did not have the courage to do, or say, otherwise.

Finding the courage to say I will no longer allow anyone to disrespect me, bully me, or threaten me into submission is the single most powerful action I have ever taken. Our words have immense power to hurt and to heal. Use that power wisely.

END WHITE SILENCE

You ask me to tell you of my experiences
You – who want to assist me, but insist it is I who must lead

To speak of my experiences
in classrooms with white students supported by you

Curious about my presence

What did she do to get here?
How, and why is she here?
Knowing with all their finite wisdom that I cannot be
as qualified as others

To tell you
You – whose children address me by my first name
A missed opportunity
The black woman
Always giving everything
Except the directives

Explain to you how I am treated in your absence
Do you not talk of me?
Hear the conversations?
About the b_ _ _ _ that dared to assign a grade
less than what they felt they deserved,
by their estimation – lacking degree # 1
And now
not even the traditional accoutrements of being educated

Challenging me for acting as if I am in control,
the one who did not teach what they decided was expected
I do not act as they think I should
I am an educated "uppity n_ _ _ _ _" not knowing my place
They will not address me with any appropriate salutation

Me who writes poetry…
You cannot control my forum, nor genre
Having learned the other ways of knowing on the long road to the
back door

The marginalized – they are the majority,
usher in the new paradigms and creative methodologies

Explain how I am treated in your absence?

Do you not see me?
How others make their observations
The surprise as I walk into the room
An unexpected guest
What is it that she does to her hair?

You want to support me in every way that you can
Asking me for directions
Dismissing the subtle – obvious truths

You who have not engaged with me about qualitative methodology
The assumptions
My lacking a serious review of the literature,
placing the method before the thought –
Always the flaw of more dominant ways of knowing

You who offers suggestions on my practice
…from the exterior of my classroom
having such faith in the quibbles of poorly prepared students

You have yet to read my work,
but underestimate my capabilities

Talk plain to me,
that you will do everything you can to support me,
except confront white privilege

The blonde/brunette pony tails, clean cuts
are never contested by one of color
The credentials, status, nor blood sweat and tears withstanding

Students who first complain
Then lie

I smile, strange
Thinking of all the dead black men who never saw her face,
Desired her womanhood
The unfulfilled suggested criminal acts
Doing hard time,
For being at the wrong place at the wrong time

OJ will pay for being able to act like a white man
Within the silence - Hedda,
may you find your face

There were no cries to end domestic violence for you

Still – a white woman can kill her babies,
she said she saw a black man

Were the slave ships not enough?
Genocide
Today it's
Oklahoma
Rosewood
and
Special Education

The student said I drew blood,
pushed her
called them racists
she made a mistake
the story was not accurate

As inaccurate as it would be if a black male said the same to Mr.
Charlie,
and us believing he would never pay for his mistake

Mothers begin to hide their dark sons when the story is
misunderstood
They know the seriousness of inaccuracies
Dumb ignorance
Emmett may you rest in peace
Dr. Cameron
The voice of a dead man

Here I am BA, MS, SAS, CAS, PD, Ed.D., MBA on the way
Excuse me miss
And your qualifications are ???

Always the assumption of what I am not

Oh excuse me... I thought you worked here
I thought you were a student
I didn't realize you were on faculty
Do you have your degree?
Oh, excuse me... you're Dr. Wattsjohnson!

Always the assumptions
Thinking to know what I am
Candidate for intimacy with any black male within the circle
Closely aligned with "black culture"
Unlike the rest, because of your fascination with who I am

Living in a community by choice
Owning a home ???
Independent
Individualized
Well read
Interest aside from "black stuff"

I ask myself where the smile comes from
Withstanding the quizzes
All with the same question

How did you get to be as normal as me?

I hear you saying that you want to help,
but we need to begin with my humiliation
The first time being only about practice, not theory

In my absence how would injustice be dealt with?
Oh... excuse me
I think I understand

Double standard, lip service, status quo… grin and bear it come to mind

You sit and listen intently
Surprised at the complexities which you created

What do you tell your children when I am not there?

End your silence

Now we begin

End White Silence is an essay about coping with racism within academia and is the published work of which I am most proud. It begins with a poem inspired by the queries of colleagues who wanted to better "understand" my experiences with discrimination. We were part of a university that talked a lot about their belief in working "for social justice." Although they marginalized me, my work and my experiences, they still spoke about wanting to better "understand" the work of social justice by having me do the talking. You know what they say... be careful what you ask for.

End White Silence explored the reality of existing at a predominately white institution from the perspective of a black woman. The issues range from the complexities of collegial relationships with authentic voice, the power of white students when dealing with faculty of color and the mixed messages I received from a supportive administration. It also referenced the social and political climate of the black experience with white power in the United States, demonstrating how history informs the present.

The poem and essay is entitled "End White Silence," for it begins and ends by suggesting to whites who encourage "others" to tell their stories of injustice, that they are the ones who need to speak first. What follows is the majority of the original article that was published in Multicultural Perspectives in 2003 with some revision.

This essay has been part of my thought processes for the last five years, but in the making, more realistically for the last 30 years. I have accumulated the incidents that have lead to this essay since I have had the ability of recall. I address what I believe is the most evasive impediment to resolving issues of race in America -- white silence.

White silence, simply stated, is when a person who identifies with "being white" and/or "looks white," is silent in the face of injustice. White silence in the face of injustice, maintains the status quo and attributes power to those already in power, and marginalizes those who are not. Because of the latter, all individuals, whites and people of color help to maintain the power structure that already exists and can participate in white silence. In this essay, I express my experience as a black woman inside the academy to end my participation in the silence. My inspiration comes from the many incidents where white colleagues ask me to explain my experiences so they might better understand my struggles with racism. I begin with an interpretation of key terminology, and then proceed with an explanation of some ideas expressed in the poem.

The Language We Use

Because language and our use of it is always in a state of evolution, and a place of struggle over our intended meaning, I will state my present position regarding my interpretation of the terms: black, white, people of color and minority.

In our North American society, whether spoken or unspoken, things are thought of, and acted upon, in terms of being black or white. When I use the term black to describe others and myself, I am tapping into a shared experience of what it is like to exist as a black person in America. Situating myself as a black woman also associates me with the reality of what my past, present and future experiences have been and will likely be in this society. I will also use the term African American. When I use this term, it is in reference to my sense of who and what I am; the ancestry and rich history from which I have evolved, versus the reality of my negative experiences as a black person in America.

The term white, besides referring to a community of individuals, also represents an inequitable, unjust and exploitative system of power in America. It speaks about "the haves" versus "the have nots," and those individuals the United States has established as the norm. It is because the term white does the latter so well, that it makes sense for me to use it with great intention.

When I speak about the institution at which I work as being predominately white, or refer to white colleagues, I am referring to all of the above. It is important to me, and hopefully my colleagues, that we are aware of the different realities that exist for each of us within academia. My use of the term colleague refers to anyone with whom I have contact while engaging in professional activities (e.g., you as the reader of this essay). It does not solely refer to the colleagues with whom I work on a weekly basis.

When I use the term people of color, I do not wish to heighten the division between individuals of color and those who are white, but to acknowledge and talk about the clearly defined line that exists in American society. I believe that as human beings we all have color, and that the essence of what we are is not black, white or otherwise. But that is not what I am trying to emphasize when I use the term people of color. When I use the term, people of color, I refer to the way we have socially constructed ourselves within this society and the power relationships that accompany that construction. The term people of color refers to all those who do not share in the privileges and advantages of being white within our society.

For all of my professional life, I have resisted the term minority because it categorically speaks untruth about who and what I am. The use of the term minority is a powerful component of white silence. Minority is defined as the condition, or fact of being smaller, inferior or subordinate (Oxford English Dictionary). When the term minority is used in reference to individuals in our society, it implies the above definition about those who are defined as such, or whatever it is used to describe. I am opposed to the use of the term minority when referring to people. When I hear people refer to others, or me, as a minority, it is a subtle reminder of our suggested "place" within this society that we must actively resist.

The term underrepresented is preferable to me, because of the political consequences that accompany it. Referring to me as an underrepresented scholar within American universities, says that I am not well represented, but that I need to be. No one is calling me less than. Instead, I hear a desire to include the viewpoints of underrepresented scholars that have not been part of the larger discussion, and to broaden the perspectives we hold within academia. It is with this intention that I proceed.

The Intention

In this essay I seek to take the concept of what is like to be a black woman at a white institution and present it as a lived experience. In doing this I provide an opportunity for the discussion to occur on topics on which my white colleagues are silent. I speak about topics that are part of our silenced dialogue to create an opportunity for honest reflection. To do this well, I have found creative expressions, such as poetry and a free flow of prose useful.

Writing is a revelatory means of academic expression that allows me to connect with the essence of my thoughts. Once these ideas are on paper, I can step back with a critical intellectual lens to analyze the realities and the contradictions. "End White Silence" was a flow of consciousness that allowed me to process the difficult experiences that occurred during my first year at a new institution. I also believe introducing artifacts, such as the ones I share in this essay, are necessary to paint an accurate account of my reality [1].

Collegial Relationships

Too often when I connect with colleagues to challenge injustice in our world, it begins with their desire for me to articulate my own personal struggle. This has become passé. Asking me to begin the conversation by talking about the injustices I have experienced removes the burden for them to speak about the injustices they have helped to perpetuate. It suggests that they do not see the problems in which they are active participants. It also subtly suggests that I am the problem as if "the problem" did not exist before I arrived. This is not the case. The problem of systemic racism within American universities exists whether an institution has faculty of color or not, so the conversation, and the work, to change the system can convene without our presence.

Many of my interactions at the university revolve around how I arrived here. These interactions suggest that there is something rare and uncommon about a black woman being where I am with the dispositions and abilities I possess. There is surprise when I exhibit characteristics of leadership that I believe should be expected of anyone similarly positioned. I have a doctorate in educational policy and leadership studies and have worked in the field of education for over 20 years. I am now in a tenure-track position as a member of a faculty in a department that prepares future school leaders. It strikes me as odd when other professionals are surprised to observe that I write well, am politically astute and have some understanding of the complexities and nuances of scholarly research. On these occasions, I wonder if these individuals can recognize their own prejudices exhibited by their lower expectations for me.

The consistent breach of etiquette and the liberties that are taken when addressing and referring to women and people of color continue to be a disappointment. Colleagues whom I, and others address as doctor or professor in all professional circumstances, introduce me to their school age children, other students and colleagues as Yolanda. When this occurs I find myself questioning their depth of understanding of the political and social context within which we operate. Why are the rules of etiquette relaxed when dealing with me? Introducing me as who I am, Dr. Wattsjohnson removes the onus from the person being introduced to me and thus the responsibility of determining how I am situated within the university. This is significant for it is far from the norm that African American women are perceived as scholars within the academy.

On one occasion during a tour of a school building with colleagues, I was introduced as "Ms.", while each of my colleagues were introduced as "Dr." to a classroom of students. The negative ramification of this incident was that the children did not have an opportunity to see me, a black woman, as a doctor. The black children missed the opportunity to view me as a role model of what they could one day become, and the white children did not have the experience of hearing a black woman addressed in a manner that is most often reserved for white men. Given that I was the only black woman in the group, it confirmed the inappropriate socially constructed notion that I was the least significant member in the group. As I reflect on these incidents I am deeply saddened to recognize how deeply rooted the disassociation with black women as scholars remain. Black women are not regularly seen as being part of the academy; making the shift to consciously address me as a scholar seem odd, while doing so is consciously and unconsciously resisted.

The silencing and refusal to accept me as a scholar of equal and very capable intellectual capacity is a constant tension I experience when dealing with colleagues. In a discussion with a colleague about my research interest, I was asked if I had yet to do my review of the literature. I expressed that I was still in the rudimentary conceptual stages and had yet to review the literature, for a starting point of research often begins with an examination of the researchers' own lived experience (Clandinin & Connelly, 1994). My colleague suggested that I should read what others had to say before I continued. After this conversation, a different colleague engaged me in a discussion about how I might go about doing a review of the literature for a possible joint research project, yet he never followed up with the research interest.

Through the power of suggestion I was placed in the position of proceeding incorrectly within the paradigm of my choice. It appeared to me that my colleagues were checking to see if I understood the importance of a review of the literature without honestly engaging me in a discussion of the conceptualization of my research. It was implied that I might not know what I was doing.

I now understand that sometimes when colleagues ask me "what do you think" I am not really being asked what I think, as much as they are probing to see if I am thinking as they think I should.

White Students Versus Faculty of Color

Not only are my capabilities as a researcher questioned without much forethought, but my abilities as a classroom practitioner are questioned as well. After a semester of listening to the complaints of students, one of the administrators at my institution, offered to sit down and talk with me about some of the ways I could improve my practice based on what he had heard from students. He did not understand that I interpreted his offer as an acceptance that he believed problems existed within my practice that needed to be corrected. Neither did he understand my disappointment with his conclusions that were based on student complaints. He felt I should be open to receive his suggestions, and that I should not be defensive about my practice [ii].

This scenario is a powerful example of how the power of whiteness operates within the academy. By merely suggesting their disapproval, my white students were able to create an unsatisfactory image of my teaching abilities. The silenced part of this dialogue is the tendency to give more weight to the complaints of white students about a professor of color, than is normally given to complaints about white faculty members. White faculty members may also be subjected to student complaints at inappropriate levels within the institution, but they do not have the same sustained weight. Complaints about white faculty are dismissed more readily than when the faculty member in question is a person of color. The students are not afforded the same sense of agency when dealing with white faculty members. Similar to the norms of etiquette for introductions that were referred to earlier in this essay, the rules of etiquette for communication with a professor are relaxed when white students are dealing with faculty of color.

When some of my students received a grade they felt was inappropriate, they reacted by speaking to one of my white colleagues. They were dealing with the anger of being poorly assessed by someone they felt was inferior to them; they sought to remedy the situation by soliciting the assistance of a white colleague. They perceived my white colleague as having the power to "put me in my place."

My desire is to move away from the paternalistic relationships where I am asked to explain why the disrespect I have experienced at the whim of white students is unjustified; it is an ultimate form of professional humiliation. It should behoove white colleagues who allow students to speak to them about a colleague of color before the student has spoken to the professor, to examine themselves and their motives [iii]. Do they want to help, or do they believe, as their actions suggest, that the colleague in question does not merit the same level of respect and dignity that they themselves expect from students and other colleagues?

How History Informs the Present

Sadly, through the power of suggestion and the use of accusation (often lies) by whites against blacks in the United States, whites can still wreak unavoidable havoc in our lives. The following is the exact text of an e-mail exchanged between two administrators at my institution. I was asked to respond to the accusations. The use of all names, except for my own, have been replaced with *****.

*****,

*I just completed a phone call with an upset parent, *****. She was attempting to reach you but I took the call in your absence.*

*Mrs. ***** was calling about Dr. Wattsjohnson. The following are points from our conversation.*

*Her daughter, *****, had just called her crying. This has happened before. During (after) class today ***** picked up a paper. Yolanda grabbed *****'s hand and told her that she should not have picked it up. Yolanda's nail dug into *****'s hand and drew blood. According to Mrs. ***** there was no ill intent in picking up the paper.*

*At the same time there was another girl there and Yolanda pushed her. This girl is also calling her mother about the incident. According to *****, Yolanda has stated that "most kids here are racist". She often refers to Blacks. Also, ***** claims that Yolanda has stated that she is here to get tenure and that the kids want to get her fired.*

Recently, Yolanda failed ******'s group in a group project. According to her mother ***** has been an A or AB student.

Mrs.***** responding to her daughter during an earlier conversation suggested that she (*****) should try to meet with Dr. Wattsjohnson apart from class and talk with her about her concerns. ***** made an appointment with Yolanda who said she would give ***** 15 minutes. However, ***** was 5 minutes early and Yolanda was 10 minutes late. Yolanda only spent 5 minutes with *****.

***** has spoken with her Advisor, *****, and was told that there was nothing she could do.

Mrs.***** is a graduate of our university and enjoyed her experience here. She wants her daughter to also have a good experience (which has been the case until now).

Mrs.***** wants to know what she should do or what can be done. She doesn't want her daughter to fail and become disenchanted with our university. I told her that I would share this information with you and that you would get back to her. She may be reached at:
******

*****

She will be home Friday and back at work on Monday.

Please keep me advised.

******

Putting a face on my reality by providing specific content helps the reader better understand what it means for me to exist at a predominately white institution, and to move beyond a conceptual conversation of my reality.

My response to the document was that it was pure hyperbole. I sought legal consul, and prayed that the truth would be revealed. After further investigation I received the following memo two months later, after insisting that I have a written statement verifying that the incident never occurred.

By this memo, we are communicating our administrative response to the matters itemized in certain notes that memorialize a telephone conversation between a parent and ***** (you have a copy of these notes). Those notes were provided to ***** by ***** following the conversation with Mrs. *****. In talking both with the student named and with you, we have discovered that the incident outlined in #2 did not occur as communicated by Mrs. *****. In particular, the student confirmed that the facts as reported by the parent were not accurate. Furthermore, it appears that the remaining points outlined in these notes are matters which should be resolved between the instructor and the student. Consequently, we decline to intervene in this matter and find that the parent call provides no basis for us to become involved at this point.

This is yet another example of the power of suggestion by a white student against a black faculty member. At one point a white colleague who was supportive of me suggested, I believe as a comforting measure, that things were not as serious as they seemed. What I could not find the words to ask him at that time was, how could a black person in America, be accused of assaulting a white person and not take it seriously?

My experience led me to reflect on the O.J. Simpson trail. What white America was most angry about was that a black man might have done what he was accused of doing to a white woman and get away with it. Black America was cheering the fact that a black man, guilty or not, was not convicted with insufficient and faulty evidence. On both sides, the loss of life was deluded in the fanfare. Our national outrage was equally lacking in the death of "Little Lisa" Steinberg in the domestic violence case of Hedda Nussbaum and Joel Steinberg (New York Times).

White silence keeps us from addressing the fact that rich privileged white men in America are able to exploit the legal system on a daily basis to their advantage. When a person of color is accused of a wrongdoing there is a tendency for whites to become silent in the presence of fellow white vigilantes. This weakens the level of trust that black Americans can reasonably have of white Americans who say they support a just society.

In the case of Susan Smith[iv], the amount of time that transpired before it was realized that she was not telling the truth about the disappearance of her children is unnerving. In actuality she had killed them herself. What is more frightening is that Susan Smith knew her chances of getting away with her crime were greater if she implicated a "black man" in the wrong doing.

The burnings and deaths that demolished the prosperous black community in Tulsa, Oklahoma, 1921 (Franklin, 1982) were ignited by the suggestion of injustice towards whites by blacks, as well as, the burnings and deaths in the destruction of Rosewood, Florida (D'Orso, 1996). In Rosewood, a white woman said that a black man tired to rape her. After the destruction of the entire town, it was revealed that the woman had lied. In actuality she had been beaten by her white lover, but wanted to hide her indiscretion from her husband.

In New York City where black boys make up a disproportionate number of all students in special education programs, I have witnessed white teachers successfully assign black male students to a special education program, because the teacher lacked support and proper classroom management skills.

As a black American I, and many members of our community know the power and danger of accusations by whites against blacks. I know that I had no choice but to take seriously the power and reality of the student's accusations. History has proven that I could not afford not to. Emmett Till (Teaching Tolerance, 1989) did not live to regret speaking to a white woman; while Dr. James Cameron, the only person known to survive a lynching has dedicated his life to telling his story with the founding of America's Black Holocaust Museum.

There are constant reminders that my education can change who I am as a person, and how I feel about myself, but it will not change the insults I am subjected to by people who choose to associate me with a history of oppression. Because of the color of my skin, I am constantly subjected to negative stereotypes that some believe should hold true for me as a black woman in America. As an academic inside the academy I am not immune to, nor protected from this form of discrimination and injustice.

As a black woman struggling for respect within the academy on a daily basis with students, colleagues and the administration, I have created a disposition that reflects confidence, capacity and strength. It is my belief that I am perceived as strong and oddly composed in the face of some of the adversity that I must deal with. The question I ask myself about my smile is just that, a question I ask in that rare moment when I stop long enough to realize how painful the work in which I am engaged in is. I wonder to myself how I do it. As any person, of any race, who struggles against an injustice knows, the work is much more difficult that our dispositions reflect. In my effort to combat systemic racism within the academy and society, I suppress the painful reality of the insults I confront. I choose to ignore the fact that too many people do not see me as a full person worthy of respect.

My poem ends with a call for white colleagues to reconsider how they "help" and support me within the academy. Working together to remove the barriers that exist for faculty of color cannot begin with my humiliation and with me silently living through experiences of discrimination and prejudice. As a black woman within the academy, I cannot be one of the few to name injustice. If we seek social justice in our world, it will mean speaking up in the face of injustice, no matter who the perpetrators are, particularly when they are white and in proximity to hear you. Although the comments made to me in private by white colleagues and students speaking out against injustice are spoken with sincerity, they are part of the silenced dialogue that is ineffective in the shadow of injustice. If we are going to continue to struggle together to make a difference to change our world, we must END WHITE SILENCE, and speak out against injustice in public places.

As a junior faculty member in any institution -- predominately black or white -- I realize that by naming the behaviors that challenge the white power structure of the American university, I place myself at risk. I also realize that if we are to advance our struggle for a more socially just world within the academy, my silence serves no one. I have chosen to pursue the path of breaking the silence and naming the behaviors that have adversely affected me. I desire conversations, actions and opportunities for real social change. In doing this I demonstrate my internalization of the lesson I learned from the late scholar Audre Lorde; "Your silence will not protect you." And so it is.

References

Clandinin, D.J., & Connelly, F.M. (1994). Personal experience methods. In Denzin & Lincoln (Eds.) Handbook of qualitative research. (413-427)
Thousand Oaks: Sage.

D'Orso, M. (1996). Like judgment day: The ruin and redemption of a town called rosewood. New York: G.P. Putnam's Sons.

Franklin, J. L. (1982). Journey toward hope: A history of blacks in Oklahoma.
Oklahoma: University of Oklahoma Press.

Oxford English Dictionary. London: Oxford University Press

The Faces of Hedda Nussbaum (1997, March 30). The New York Times

Bullard, S. (1989). Free at last: A history of the civil rights movement and those who died in the struggle. Montgomery, Alabama: Teaching Tolerance.

Walsh, C.E. (1991). Pedagogy and the struggle for voice: Issues of language, power, and schooling for Puerto Ricans. New York: Bergin & Garvey.

Notes:

ii This is not meant to be judgmental. This is difficult work that is impossible to do without uncomfortable moments. I do not name some of the unfavorable experiences I have had to blame any of the participants. I recall them so we might learn from them. I have not used names and have changed any details that would identify specific individuals. Although we do not mean to harm others with our some of our behaviors, that does not change the reality of the harm we inflict with our actions.

iii I am not questioning the need for evaluations by colleagues as part of my professional growth. I am questioning the assumptions of deficits that exist in my practice by colleagues unfamiliar with my work.

iv By entertaining complaints about me without advising students to speak to me, my colleagues reinforce the students predisposition not to respect me as they do other members of the faculty. It minimizes the amount of respect they feel is necessary when confronting a difficult situation with a black professor.

v In 1994, Union, South Carolina, Susan Smith strapped her two sons into their car seats and rolled the car into a lake. She told police that a black man had carjacked her 1990 Mazda with her sons still in the car. After a nationwide search, nine days later, she confessed to her crime.

SISTERS READING SISTERS*

We will tell the story in black and white
until years from now it has a happy ending

Let us begin to tell the story the way we want to tell it
One of love and hope
Abundance for us
Our children

What is this?
The black woman being the mentor to the world
I know the pain of the burden
I wonder what you suppress in your silence
Do you bear a cross for all the thank yous [sic] that have never
been said?

Yea though I walk through the valley of the shadow of death,
I fear no evil
For thou art with me

Who else is there to lean on?
Walking out into the world
Afraid of the elements of evil

Let us fight outgrowing our humanity into the color of our skins

Do not fear our coping mechanisms
-- the laughter
You cannot understand, nor take it all

Thankful to white woman who see reality
Others
Treating the blackness of our children
and their mommas -- as destructive forces

Well meaning white people that do not trouble the tenacious bar-
rier between us
I will not be invited to dinner
To lunch
Your home
Birthday parties
Pot lucks or fish fries
No place –
where the neat barriers are not well maintained
Relatives that might slip
Do slip
You cannot disagree with them
You tell me more by not inviting me

Talk to them girlfriend
Why is it that white folks leave the discussion of racism to blacks...
if they are the experts???

The black women here today will benefit from the gift of
conversation

Not talking about it
Means doing nothing about it
Talking about it is doing something about it

I too know the resolve
Can't be friends with a white girl
They always get around to calling you by the "n" word
They will have lunch without me
Look uncomfortable when everything that I need to know is
revealed

I'll clarify your fixation with the "n" word
Don't

In my generation,
We can never be
don't want to be
close enough for you to use the term with me
In any context
Under any circumstance
For any reason
And particularly... NOT by accident

But we use it ???
Then wait until you become black for your turn...
to use a word that degrades us all

Tired of the hurt of vulnerability
Thinking it was safe to trust you

Two steps forward
ten steps back
I refuse to explain it to you
Find another exotic black girl to be your friend

I will not do the hair thing
Wanting to quantify the number of "accidental touches"
How you degrade me
Do you also want to inspect my teeth?

When I was ten years old and my new word for the week was
"accidentally"
On use # 5
My mother let me know that the next time I did something
"accidentally"
She would "accidentally" my behind
Sometimes
There is nothing like a consequence to prevent accidents

Is there a white sister out there brave enough to be real?

The commonality of pain
Why is it a shared misery?
Learning of poor little white girls who fought their uncles off
But calling each other by mean names

Pain festers and grows
Hold onto the love of children that promise to write every day
Even a little white girl that doesn't know her letters

Tina was able to teach us too much
Passed down with unspoken lessons
If Tina can get away from Ike
Can we get away from the racism that separates us?

What story will you tell when you go home?
Will you admit/remember
Rosewood and Tulsa when they say we exaggerate
If you need a -- but this is now
Talk to me

How can the stories we share today free us from the past?
Leading us to a gray truth
What are our common ghosts?

Can we deal with lesbian lovers?
From Milwaukee
Loving across boundaries of race
A multiplicity of broken taboos
Teaching us how to raise our children
Reminding us how to love
Not needing to make everything all right
Going the distance

White sisters is there truth in the accusations that you cannot to be
counted on?
Are you truly one-dimensional?
Not being able to confront both race and white male supremacy

How can we be an America with pride for freedom and justice?
Suppressing the middle ground
Is there new ground to support us?
Their are no winners or losers in this dialogue

We will push the boundaries where we find them
They are all over
Resist the everyday stereotyping that tatters the soul
And -- it – happens -- every -- day

Are there dissenters in the room?
Can you learn how to be?
Will you endure outsider status?
Is it more important to fit in?

Eating cheese and sipping wine
How do you not chock?
Humorless... the off color jokes
The loudness of what is not said
Is deafening
The lack of textured visibility
Strain the eye

If sisterhood is earned and not proclaimed
How will we earn our stripes?

Please do not offer yourselves as sacrificial lambs
Black men trying to "f - - -" their way to revenge

Women know that revenge is an empty concept
Work to heal your wounds
The oppressor and the oppressed both become bruised

How do we all hide behind the intellectual shoe polish?
Use the intellect to read
Learn the experiences of others
Encounter a breath and appreciation for the range of the black
experience
No peace
But greater understanding

Work to know my story as I know yours
Fed to me via years of formal education

Honor people of color for the depth and challenge of our education
Consuming the knowledge of white supremacy
In our larger moments
Forced to seek knowledge of ourselves in the dim light before days
begin
and end

Are we women that engage and enrage our students?
Our children
Our families
To learn
Triggering within them an unstoppable urge for knowledge
Preferably about something that might change their lives

Life must be a learning experience
Studying the past
Struggling in the present
Charting the future of race relations in America

Black women, just doing their best
Confronting extraordinary obstacles
To have an ordinary life

Let's talk about the truth of the matter
Everyone's ancestors came out of Africa
There is a gene of an ancient African woman in us all,
This explains our incomprehensible ability to love all of humanity

Let me say that again
There is a gene of an ancient African woman in us all,
This explains our incomprehensible ability to love all of humanity

Others who willingly offer covert support
This gets in the way
Helps no one

Today will you admit to at least one scary thought in public?
Can you hear just one scary thought in public?
Neither lashing out at the other
Just letting the words hold their own space
There is such beauty in the silence once true words have been spoken

We will struggle to be productive
Expecting disagreement and a little scorched earth
But we must persist
Lets promote a groundswell for political incorrectness,
Making mistakes
Learning from them
Show your true colors
Whatever your color

Black women have been the forerunners
Leading to benefits for white women
Will you share the proceeds?
We are not ungrateful for white women making abortion legal for
themselves
No longer needing to mutilate our innards
With sisters
And dirty doctors that promised peace of mind

Then there is the question of truth
The litmus test
What assurance do we have that Miss Ann will want to share what-
ever advantage she gains with us?
Does she really want us to have the kind of power we want for
ourselves?

What is your level of discomfort as an intelligent beautiful black
woman stands before you?
Responsible for convening this conversation
Having insight and courage beyond my years

Will you be able to support me?
Love me?

Let us not just talk the talk, but also
Walk the walk
Together

Do not underestimate my political acumen
Respect that I do understand
Much – more – than – you -- realize
Know the power of my political actions
This action
This conversation
Sister Reading Sisters

Having gracefully removed the sign marked "whites only"
Women of color are no longer seeking entry
You are invited to come in
We will walk truth through the door holding hands
Or we will never find our strength to walk at all

I will hold the space
Helping us
Manage conflict
Re-conceptualize power
While creating a spirit of community

Get ready for the sweetness of understanding power
The heartbeat of our movement

Affirming unprecedented love and solidarity
Between black and white women
All women

Sisters Reading Sisters is a dialogue about our similarities
We know the differences
They remain
Pieces of a beautiful quilt

We will not construct a conceptualization of our issues as all or
nothing
We will not see pass the impossible issues of race
We cannot deny they exist

We will create a community where we can trust each other
Go the journey
Resolve issues of conflict and disappointment
Including our anger with each other

Use this space to openly express your deepest yearning for a true
sisterhood
Rebuking the truth of how we have internalized our struggles
Wrestled inwardly
All by ourselves
Alone
with our choices
with our fears
This will not define our womanhood

So let us join hands
Hearts
Minds
And desires

Metaphorically
Physically
Spiritually
Forging a sisterhood of women
That READ, SPEAK and ACT
To change our lives and the lives of others

Ashay
Yolanda M. Wattsjohnson
February 26, 2003

* A collage of text inspired by <u>Skin Deep:Black and White Women Write About Race</u>
Edited by Marita Golden and Susan Richards Shreve

Ten years ago I wrote Sisters Reading Sisters for a research endeavor I began in Milwaukee, Wisconsin, while a professor at Marquette University. My desire, as is the case with all my community engagement work, was and is to move people past the stage of conversation and verbal apology. We must change our own lives first and then our interactions with each other.

To facilitate this process I began a project using the book <u>Skin Deep: Black Women & White Women Write About Race</u>, by Marita Golden and Susan Richards Shreve. Each woman who signed up to participate in the project was given a copy of the book to read and committed to participating in a discussion with all the other women over the course of two events. This piece of prose was the opening introduction for the project.

Writing the prose for the project was in and of itself a form of catharsis and therapy. Knowing that I would share the work with others as the professor leading the project required that I be candid about some of the very things we are more comfortable hiding behind. It was liberating. To begin the process of an authentic healing of women between the color lines, I had to completely surrender the false security of being comforted within my silence. I had to model my hopes and dreams.

When I presented this work it felt uncomfortably long to read. It was a long piece because I was set on weaving in some aspect of each chapter of the book. This was the first time I took an entire book, a chapter book no less, and wove it into a piece for spoken word. Given the context, one of my greatness concerns was that I might not touch upon a sentiment from the book that a sister in the audience would need to hear.

The second phrase of the project, Sisters Reading Sisters, which did not occur then, but has occurred with the publication of this book, <u>For the Sake of My Sanity: One Woman's Journey of Speaking Truth to Power and Ignorance</u>, is the inauguration of a global book club of sisters reading sisters. Together we will simply read a book written by a sister telling her story and commit to speak about that truth with another sister. Simple, yet powerful. I hope you will JOIN US at:

SistersReadingSisters.com

The words of Audre Lorde always come to mind, "Your silence will not protect you."

GRANDPARENT'S LOVE

Childhood, the gift, if you are lucky,
...cause the rest may not work out so good
True coming of age is
Fighting
Meanness
Jealousy
Abuse
Neglect
Get over on you
Pretend to be your friends
Hating your light
Wanting to see you fail
Angry when you don't
Always being told what's wrong with you... everyday
Words that stab, then cut, deep
deeper...
Enjoy childhood

If you've been so blessed
Eat with your grandma and grandpa
You are their bright little thing
They never say "I love you"
Why bother...
Feel the smile and warmth in their eyes
Laughing with you
Not too much hugging and kissing
It's of no use
I already know you love me
and keep kissing you anyway
There is no place to hide... and they never push me away

A spoken testament of affection
Might spoil the sensation
Magic is never explained

Grandma's food speaks volumes
Grandpa says nothing
He is just always there... next to her
He always does, giving so much you never have to ask
Older, I understand that he was just "being" a man
Real men need not proclaim their manhood

The pain of what I miss, is often greater than the suffering I have
had to endure without them...

Unconditional love...
Preparing me, yet leaving me unprepared to live without them

My grandparent's love was and remains the blood of my life. If it were not for the love in which they enveloped me... and my writing, I would have died shortly after my grandfather made his transition. At times I wonder about the lesson God wants to teach me by having me live in what I often experience as a loveless world without them. This topic is challenging to write about because all that I would relate to you, has only been felt in every cell of my body. I have never had any words that can express how I feel and felt about my grandparents. *"Grandparent's Love"* is my inadequate attempt to express the role they played in my life.

Actually, as I become more mature and get closer to entering the age when we first met, I understand and love them even more. You do not understand the love I already profess for them, so to say I am learning to love them even more, amazes even me.

They were my light in some vey dark places that for the time being, and hopefully forever, have been erased from my memory. I think the best I can do is to write about the type of grandparent I hope to be someday and speak about them as I explain what I believe my role will be. For starters I have decided I will not be called "Grandma," for me it's Sunshine. That is what I want to be for all the children in my life and what I feel my grandparents were to me. They were, and are still the light of my life. When I am sad, which I am less prone to be of late, but have been the majority of my life, if I think of my grandparent's love; just like the sun, it comforts me with a ray of warmth and love.

Sunshine is also the name that random strangers have been most prone to give me. Just this year a man passing me while I worked in my garden blessed me when he said,

"Okay Sunshine, there you go, just look at you, just spreading your love!"

It was a magical moment for me because I had recently been grappling with what I would allow my children (I had a failed adoption attempt of my son, Robert) and grandchildren to call me. My commitment to all children, but especially the babies I will grand-parent, is to protect them the way my grandparents protected me. Allowing my grandchildren to call me Sunshine will be my tribute to my grandparents and a small reminder that loving children profoundly is life's most important action.

My grandparents conditioned me, without ever saying a word, that true love is best demonstrated, not spoken.

Recently, I adapted the stance that any person that claims to love me should "act" as if they love me, instead of merely loving me. This is powerful. When I state that someone should "act" like they love me, I do not have to argue with anyone about whether they are loving me or not. As long as they "act" like they love me I can be content. I am clear that acting like you feel a certain way, takes precedence over your words stating how you feel.

This concept has been instrumental for me in my work with children. Instead of criticizing their personhood, I make clear the type of behaviors (the way you act) that I expect from them. When they are less than appropriate I begin my scolding with something like, "I love you to pieces, but in this moment you are acting like someone I do not want to be around." My caution to you, if you want to use this idea with children, is to carefully select your words. I caught myself at one point saying, "I still love you, but...." This is a conditional statement because of the word still. When I used the word still, I was saying that for the moment you still have my love, but maybe there is a chance of you losing it if you do not behave in a certain way.

This was me repeating some of the same trauma I experienced as a child and as an adult. It was clear to me at a very young age that if I acted a certain way, never cried and pretended that I was okay with whatever was being said or done to me, then it was more likely that my abuser would "talk nice" to me, and thus from a child's perspective, "act like" they loved me. If I did not do as they wanted, or expressed any disagreement with them, then they would not "act" as if they loved me.

Without realizing it, regrettably as a child I made myself responsible for others' expression of love towards me, especially those that dealt with me in an abusive manner. If they did not "act" like they loved me, it was because of something I did, or did not do, as they expected and thus lead to me not being loved.

This, the concept that actions speak louder than words, has enabled me to make sense of a lot of situations that have not measured up. Any person interacting with me, should act as they wish to be perceived. If we say we are good friends, then may your actions demonstrate that. If you are a good man seeking my attention, say nothing, but smother me with the actions that say, "I love you," not words.

My own experiences have demonstrated that a good hint to help you determine if you are being abused is if an action which injures your spirit only occurs within the private space between you and that individual or situation. If this is the case, then there might be some abusive aspects of the relationship that need to be addressed. Yes... I do realize what I am saying. If we are being honest, it would be a challenge to find a woman, man or child on the planet that has not suffered some kind of abuse.

The good news is that I was raised by two very amazing people. We had the best of the simple and profoundly good life. My grandparents worked together to build a life which included a nice home, food and family gatherings. Not once in my life did I ever hear or see either of them disrespect the other, or did I ever feel any grudge of anger between them.

Now, don't get me wrong... my grandmomma, was the best of the old school black Southern women who could fuss you in, or out, of whatever situation was best for your well-being. The beauty of her fussing was that there was never anything ugly or hurtful on the other side. Neither of my grandparents used profanity or drank, and unkindness to anyone was just unheard of.

As my extended family continues to get smaller and my desire to be in committed relationship and part of a family goes unfulfilled, I still struggle with the sadness of not being part of a loving family unit. Strangely enough, my experience of being enveloped in my grandparent's love has simultaneously prepared me, yet has left me unprepared, to understand the world in which I now live.

WHAT AM I SO HAPPY ABOUT?

People tell me that I smile a lot
some even say I smile too much

What do I have to be sad about?
Folk don't know that my momma left my father,
before he really beat the shit out of her

Although her had the saw to her neck,
he didn't pull it across her throat to stop her from
Screaming
I was glad
cause he wouldn't do what I told him to
Stop hurting my momma

When we left
We lived with my grandma and grandpa
all-the-time

My mother and I slept in the same room on a hi-riser bed
She let me sleep on the higher bed bed and sometimes I would roll
down
and sleep right on top or her
She was warm
and snoring LOUD
I was so close I could feel the sound start down in her chest
The soft air that blew gently out of her mouth
and I stayed there.. the whole night
On weekends
I got to be with my grandma and grandpa, aunt and cousin

We always had some serious food...
And my aunt's fried chicken,
as long as she fried it hard enough
cause my grandmomma, as she told my aunt...
"don't like no half cooked chicken"
The Colonel had to get the recipe from my aunt
but he didn't make it as good

And he must not have known about my grandmomma's
macaroni and cheese, peach cobbler, stuffing (she called it dressing),
candied yams and mmmh mmmh chicken and dumplings
Cause if he wanted to get richer,
he would have begged her to show him how to do it
.... but she did it for us,
and never acted like the kids couldn't have as much as the adults
Talk -- about -- smiling

Folk don't know that same Summer we moved into our new house
I went around the corner with Eric Turner,
when I wasn't supposed to
To see the accident

The car looked just like my Uncle Benny's
and the dead man inside, just like him
When I ran around the corner to tell them there was an accident,
nobody even beat me because I had done something wrong

There is no smile here,
but we got through
For that I am grateful

Folk don't know how well I survived
The mistreatment
Suffered at the hands of some of my brothers
The sister friends that betrayed me
Family that "loves" you, but doesn't "act" like it
It builds character
Cause look at me now
Glad bout' the lessons I learned and how wise I've become
Smart enough to learn from my and others missteps

And although I go to work everyday
The knowledge of all these degrees jammed up in my head
The world and the people I work with
Still want to treat me like I am there for their entertainment

I have to smile

When they realize that I might know a little something
I smile at their discomfort

Really wanting to laugh cause they don't even know,
As my Auntie said, I'm my grandparents grand baby
and I haven't even begun to show them what I really know

The wisdom passed around the table
Having centuries of mother wit in my blood
Though the Spirit
At the stove getting my hair done
In-between my mother's legs as she pulled on the last braid
Stretching my temples further than I thought possible

I am amazed that others can live in this world and not see how beau-
tiful it is
Children... know that this is heaven,
Yet they are always telling us it's someplace else

Going to those churches where they try to squeeze GOD up there
on the podium with the minister that talks too loud
Telling me what I should do and what GOD wants for me

I just smile

I don't tell them that my momma told me I could talk to GOD for
my own self
When I am confused I can question GOD and say
"I know you GOD in all,
but something ain't right and I need you to explain it to me."

She taught me how to listen so when the answer comes
I can hear it
I am finally old enough to go deep down in my bones, knowing that
I do have everything that I need inside of me

If you want to know ecstasy
Know this
See it that won't put a smile on your face

So when people tell me that I smile a lot
The real fools say,
too often
I just smile harder
And when I'm rude...
I laugh
Spilling my smiles all over the place

I think about how good the sunshine feels on my face,
Connect with the Spirit that resides within

I found the secret to my joy
and I cannot get enough of my own smile

One of the most interesting things about my evolution to choose JOY is recognizing the resentment I pick up from some people that I am as happy as I am. This piece, "What Am I So Happy About?" is a courtesy poem to explain my happiness. At times people have been distrustful of my JOY, thinking I am feigning happiness, or just "being friendly" like folks do at a job interview, only to tire of me when they realize I am actually this way all the time. But as the title says, this book is written for the sake of my sanity. It is not about staying not happy, so that others are more comfortable with their own discomfort when they are around me.

Another aspect of this book is getting to the core of my happiness, staying there and being comfortable with it. Although I have chosen to be a happy person and exhibit that to the rest of the world, I have also hidden, more appropriately, buried, a lot of my pain and sadness on the inside. What you see on the outside is not an act, but there has been a schizophrenic aspect of my personality where I spent years, over a decade, laughing in public, only to cry myself to sleep each night.

My body has developed its own coping mechanism for dealing with all the stress in my life that I skillfully hid. The first indication of this was right after my grandmother died, the most traumatic event of my life. The day of her funeral when walking to the church my legs began to shake uncontrollably and a few days later I had my first and only major episode with gouty arthritis. For those of you that do not know about "Arthur," ... well gout is the king of pain in the arthritis family. It was discovered because one morning I awoke literally screaming because the sheet touched my foot!

Next, when my grandfather died, the evening of his funeral my legs just stopped working again. I could not walk without being supported, or exert enough pressure to operate my car. My other physical manifestations of stress are a picking of the skin on my fingers and toes that has unfortunately left those areas without pigment, classic lower back spasms which can render me unable to walk, vertigo and unknowingly nursing a bleeding ulcer for over a decade. One exciting prospect of writing this book is that I hope and believe as I release the pain... get it out of my body, these manifestations should cease.

The most recent event which proved an indication that this will be the case was my tooth episode. Around the same time that I got serious about getting this book out and letting go of harmful relationships, I had developed a boil with white puss inside my mouth. The dentist x-rayed the tooth and told me the root was infected and that the tooth needed to be removed. When it was removed the surgeon discovered that the decayed tooth had rotted so completely at the root that there was hardly any bone left. Even the doctor did not understand how someone with the good dental hygiene I had demonstrated, along with regular check-ups could have had a tooth rotted so badly without more symptoms.

Upon reflection, it made total sense to me; it was a metaphor for my life! I had hidden the negative stress of my life for so long without any outward appearance that no one, not even me, would suspect there was such deeply rooted pain in my life. Without the security that my grandparent's love provided me, a committed relationship, family or friends that consistently and unconditionally "acted" like they loved me, I was alone. The conditional "love" that at times seemingly existed in my life had been "rotten" even if it looked good on the outside.

Since my grandmother's death, my MO (modus operandi) seems to have been to deal well on the outside, only for my body to have some kind of physical manifestation of stress. Just like the deeply buried decayed roots of my tooth, I have allowed rotten emotions to have permanent residence within my body. The good news is that it is time to release it all. Writing this book is part of my detox process and healing. With it, my true self demands the release of all relationships within my life that do not allow me to practice self-love.

The irony and beautiful metaphor of the tooth episode is that throughout my life and to this day I still have strangers tell me what a nice smile and beautiful teeth I have. When someone compliments my smile I can receive it as a spiritual reminder to scan my psyche and make sure there is nothing rotten hidden beneath my beautiful smile. I always love a good metaphor, and this one, accompanied by a physical manifestation could not be better.

WHY I DON'T DATE WHITE MEN

If you ask me why I don't date white men,
then you don't know or fail to understand anything that I / our /
my people have been through.

Don't move, but listen to understand that I am not racist
brother
sister
white man
white sister

You see I know too much,
although not enough
Have read too many books,
listened to too many ole folk
ever juggle with any white man, but for so long

I have read about our beautiful dynasties, pharaohs, queens
Great centers

WE BUILT
where all higher knowledge began

Aztecs
Peruvian
Mayan civilizations
Thebes - Wasut
Egypt - Kemet
Fathers of philosophy
X
X
X
Fathers of Mythology
X
X
X
Fathers of Astronomy
X
X
X
Fathers of Medicine
X
X
X
Fathers of Mathematics
X
X
X
Indian civilization - First operation

I cannot forget my grandmother's story about when she was already
worked for less than her worth,
The white woman,

turned back the clock for an extra hour of labor
when her people had already robbed us of more than a century

I work with children who's eye's literally remind me of stars
Stars I tell you
Stars that shine over the universe that they once lived in harmony
with

I watch as those eyes become heavy
sad
tired
showing the glassiness of pain, as they are cheated... not from a better life,
but the mere chance

The system is run by the white man,
that I do not love
He who is responsible for a great deal of their social plight -- and
then asks,
why are they the way they are?

Keep your foot on my father's back
Work at my mother's spirit
You chop at my roots and then ask me...
Why am I the way that I am?

You are really beginning to think that I am a fool,
when you know
I possess that which you desire

I said listen
I did not say that I cannot love you, or never did,
but that I very consciously do not

Know your history
Know that one time I did welcome you
My graciousness
Although I was blind,
still retain a blurred vision, was the beginning of my downfall
Egypt -- Kemet -- as I called it, was MY HOME and Thebes
Columbus -- did -- not -- discover -- me
I knew who I was and was quite happy
I welcomed you and loved you,
before you decided to rudely overstay your welcome

When you came in from the cold,
I took you in with open arms
Gave you a welcome that your own mother would not
You turned on me
Took advantage of my better than good nature

Still trying to work with you because,
I know my history
You are my child
The mutant
That which reminds me of my negative side

But I choose not to love you
You have crossed the line and are fighting to retain your ill-gotten
position

You are a child that has disrespected an elder
There is no sympathy
That which bites the hand that feeds it will forever remain hungry

And brother
Do not pat me on my back and encourage me to
Speak Sister!
For you -- are the compliment of my pain

You
Who when in control of who you are and I at your side is the most
awesome being in the universe,
Refuse to stand up
Be the man, I once knew you to be

Did you know that once you could not even fathom the idea of
another man
Nor any collection of people keeping you down
The only thing you knew was how to bring yourself up

I was not the instrument of your enemy and you respected me for all
that I was

I was your life

All creation began in my womb

Sisters I know
I too am lonely
Tired
My body aches
I have chosen my path

Our wombs can be the beginning of a revolution

So do not ask me stupidness about why I do not date white men
There is a great nation waiting to be rebuilt
My man is worth the wait...
and I Am
Will always be
MOTHER OF THE EARTH

Wow... when I read this I still wonder who this young woman was and how she knew what she knew. Yes, I was and am that young mature woman, and now yet more mature woman, holding onto a youthful spirt, refusing to let go. So, the thing that I know you want to know is if I still feel the same way about dating white men. It ticks me off when you want to know something about an author and they make it hard to get to, hiding it someplace deeper in the chapter; so I will just get to it.

This is what I have always believed, even when I wrote this piece -- whenever anyone finds a person with whom they can experience real love, no matter what color it comes in, I believe that they should embrace it and never let go. My reality remains unchanged.

The majority of my interactions with both white and black men has sadly been one of dominance, control and submission. I have had to look at, imagine and read about real men without having any sustained intimate experience with them since my grandfather has died. While gracefully living my beliefs, I have been told that I intimidate men, to which my reply is always,

"I do not intimidate men... males maybe, but not men."

It has been suggested that my going to school, getting a job, keeping a job, teaching a class, buying a house, renovating a house and just going through life not asking for anyone's help... only to face rejection, has subjected me to the anger and resentment of both males and females that are not secure with themselves.

The sad part is that I only attempt to love and uplift all human beings with love and kindness. I have dealt with too many individuals, and males in dating scenarios, that have projected their insecurities onto me and found great fault with me. Instead of a willingness to love and accept me for what I am, and then to learn from our differences and grow together in spite of those differences, they have chosen abandonment.

Too many black males have been conditioned and enabled by both society and black females to walk away from their families, and just pick up someplace else. If we are to regain our strength and dignity as a black community, we must make it honorable to tell the truth and not make excuses for our males. It is dishonorable for any male to abandon his family.

There is an awkward omnipresent silence within our community that systematically ignores how low so many of our black males have sunk. Every NYC train ride or walk down a city street is an inventory of why I am without a partner. A train ride usually means males with legs spread wide open daring you to ask them to move, never giving a seat to all the females that stand, and not metaphorically, look down on our males. While walking down any street you hear and are greeted with language that once used to get bleeped from the airwaves, or put on pause by real men, only spoken among themselves; never in the presence of women and children.

As I write this I realize that some might disagree, because (hopefully) they have had other lived experiences. Thankfully, my lived experience is not the totality of all experience, just my own. For me not to share this perspective with you, would mean I felt coerced to lie about the reality of my experience dealing with males, or pretending that I do not understand my own truth. The purpose of this book is to end the silence that has oppressed me and speak my truth in the face of both power and ignorance.

Being the beautiful, intelligent, independent, loving black woman that I am should not be the stigma it has been in my life. It is my belief that I have dealt with males as romantic partners, and females as friends and family that have been in a such a place of struggle that they have not been able to "act like" they loved me, thus making a mutually loving and supportive relationship impossible.

My own healing begs that I look at this scenario and ask myself, why? Ta--dah! This self-love thing is a lot... and I mean, a lot, of hard work. My behavior has suggested that I thought I could fix and love folk into being better people. If I only showed them how much I loved them, even if it meant that I might suffer in the process, that was okay, because if I really loved them, it was worth it. Hello somebody!!! That is insane and not where I should be, if I am truly practicing self-love.

The beginning of the healing process for me is to release all the relationships in my life that do not allow me to practice self-love. The latter sentence needs to come printed with blinking neon text, so please re-read it, seeing it as a blinking neon sign, using whatever color works for you and your life.

My lack of courage, which permitted me to accept people into my world that stopped me from a practice of self-love, has contributed to every unhealthy adult relationship I have ever had. For those relationships and my part in them, I bear full responsibility. The good news is that I have now found the courage to choose how I spend my time, and with whom I will spend it.

I am a beautiful woman worthy of unconditional love, JOY and acceptance. This knowledge allows me to see that there are also many good, intelligent, kind, men in the world worthy of the same unconditional love. The men that Spirit places in my path that can offer me unconditional love and the space to practice self-love, will be the men that I will now date.

NO SALUTE

There was once a war where the soldiers were not saluted
when they came home
They went and fought with mixed emotions
Not sure
Those who they were fighting for did not support them

After the war, some stayed
They were never able to recover all the bodies
While others just left part of themselves there,
Giving a leg, arm or maybe an eye for democracy

There were no TV specials
Only the real thing,
brought into the homes of those still in the mother country

They could see how ugly war really was,
easily learning to hate the destruction of human life

When they came home,
there were no Whitney Houstons to sing their praises
No banners,
Yellow ribbons
Discount tickets to their favorite restaurant

Those that did return with their ailments
Injuries
Distracted minds (it's not easy to watch your friend blow up and
then have to search for the pieces)
Had to search for a place in society

These soldiers
Be they not proud in the eyes of their country, are asked to understand that we can no longer afford the burden of their medical
expenses
Continue never to address their pain

As we
Buried in deficits,
Roll out the red carpet and overload on yellow ribbons

Written after Project Desert Storm

This piece was written trying to make sense of the first known war I had to experience as an adult, while reflecting on Vietnam. The night we invaded Iraq is blazed onto my memory. A high school friend and I were heading to the popular, Roosevelt Field shopping mall. Feeling hip and stylish with a little money in our pocket, I drove and we had the radio on. Then it happened. The station was interpreted to announce that we had just begun a military air strike against Iraq, the country was at war. All I can remember was pulling over and both of us sobbing like two kindergarten children, neither one of us saying a word... not out of embarrassment, but having no language to comprehend what had just occurred.

Although, I was alive for the end of the Vietnam war, I was part of the generation that was taught that war, was something that had happened long ago. There was an assumption that we had moved beyond the need to ever drop bombs on any nation ever again to solve our problems or work through differences. Having that reality shattered, blown into pieces beyond comprehension, then layered against the very commercial natural of Project Desert Storm lead to this piece.

FIGHTING KINDNESS

I went to this little hick town where everyone spoke to me,
talking about "How do" and "Have a nice day."

At first I said, "Oh, how nice!" a friendly face in a strange place
But then it kept happening
The women in the store,
The man at the local gas station
I began to get suspicious and they could see it on my face

Look lady, you don't understand
I come from a place where you don't speak when spoken to and
when you do
Be sure you read between the lines

You only care about family
Either nothing or everything is local
The airport is a cab ride away and the stores basic stock are
specialties

You keep driving, because there is no where to park and if you do,
you've spent part of your week's salary

If you do decide to take on a friendly attitude, you do it only on the
weekend, when a free spirit is sometimes permissible

For me lady
You move to slow and talk like you don't think I have things to do
I'm not really glad to see you, because I don't know you and it had
never entered my mind that I might want to

I'm a cold person, from a cold place, striving to stay that way
Please keep your distance because your warmth only messes up my
bad disposition

Coming to terms with being an authentically kind and loving person is still an ongoing journey with me. This poem plays with me trying to get into the head of others and see things from their perspective. Often I say it is a good thing that I do not understand most people, at least the negative ones, because in order to see something in someone else, you must first possess it within yourself. We are all mirrors.

This is not to paint a picture that I am without attributes that need some polishing, but loving and kindness are two things I am actually quite good at. It does not serve me to be unkind to others, while learning how not to associate with others who insist on being unkind to me has been one of my toughest life lessons. My challenge has been thinking that loving someone, uneven when their actions are mean and their behavior horrible, is something I am "supposed" to endure in order to prove my love. This is absolutely ridiculous!

Some of my best self-therapy has been to just talk to myself as if I was counseling another person. In one of these conversations, I asked myself,

"If I do not require others to endure meanness and unkindness from me as a testament of their love or affection for me, why have I come to think that it is okay for others to require that of me?"

Not being able to come up with one reason that made sense was a wake-up call.

POVERTY

The times are changing at a drastic and almost irreversible pace

There has been and will always be poverty, but what we have is not poverty

Poverty speaks of people who depend on a crop as a means of survival and it fails

It speaks of people who live in bad climates and poor countries

It speaks of over populated areas where there is not enough food grown to feed the masses of people that exist

Poverty is what your family lives in when fate deals you a bad blow and the idea of rebounding is only considerable in the far future

It is when you do not have a variety of things to eat, enough extra money to be able to buy anything that is not characterized as a clearly definable necessity of life

That excludes toilet paper and under clothes

Poverty is when there is sickness killing off members of your community because there is not a trained doctor within a hundred miles from where you live

But what we have is not poverty

Poverty is not a person with a college education who is evicted from their apartment, because of something called gentrification

Forced to live with a family member or friend because they cannot find an affordable clean place to live and still be able to eat, off of ten thousand dollars a year

Poverty is not when their luck runs out where they are staying and are eventually forced to live on the streets

Poverty is not when a person over sixty-five has to sit home with an infected leg that later gets gangrene, because they cannot find a doctor who will treat them

It is not when your healthy twenty-one year old son,
goes to the emergency room crippled with severe pain,

Is refused treatment because he does not have the proper medical insurance and dies the next day at home still crippled up from the pain

That is not poverty

In a real poverty situation, you are not assured to find people motivated only by getting over on someone

People who cannot write their name and those who have no respect for themselves in matters of appearance and hygiene

You are not positive that the homeless person you just walked around sitting on the heating grate is so mentally and emotionally disturbed that help for them is more of a hope than an achievable reality

And then in a real poverty situation

One of your biggest wonders about your predicament is not if your inhumane state is somehow tied to your ethnic background and socio-economic class

No

What we have is not poverty,
where there should only be differences in people, not structured division

What we have is a system of political corruption

Euphemistically called anything from poverty to budget deficits, where those who govern provide primarily for themselves and others like them,

Keeping knowledge from the less aggressive and uninformed

Too often people are treated as homogenous groups judged by monetary social worth and ethnic background,
instead of groups of individuals with similar concerns goals and interests

There is something out of control in our society that is leaving too many of our people in prefabricated poverty, while elevating others to higher social-economic levels -- not solutions -- but change must be sort

POVERTY as it really exists is sad, but accepted as a situation uncontrollable by man while,

POLITICAL CORRUPTION is sad because it is created, controlled and perpetuated by man himself

This was one of my college coming of age pieces. As a double major in Anthropology and Urban Studies I was naturally drawn to issues of social justice and fairness. What strikes me as the saddest aspect of this piece is how timely it still is, and how far we have continued to slide backward as a nation with less and less morality.

That any elected official would want to deny any person health care benefits leaves me speechless, while I still do not understand why anyone... anyplace in the world must go hungry. When social or public projects are spoken of in terms of costing xyz million dollars, it saddens me. Many of us, although we do nothing, realize that it does not cost as much as stated and that a great portion of the money goes to support politically corrupt systems that pocket much of taxpayer's dollars and private donations.

Another quandary for me is how any person guilty of sexual misconduct can still hold public office. It blows my mind that as a public we act as if inappropriate behavior is acceptable. It signals to me that many others must also be guilty of the same; thus they are tolerant. Are we that lacking in our reasoning abilities not to question if a person cannot be faithful in a committed significant relationship, how or why should we trust them with a position of leadership in society?

This piece was penned in the early 80s, while all or most of what I refer to still exists and has only gotten worst. When I get really low thinking about how far backwards our morality as a nation seems to have slid since my childhood, I have to remember that our founding fathers were slave holders. Although, some would argue we are still engaged in a form of slavery, the good news is that at least on the books it is still illegal. So, maybe things are not as bad as they can be... we are still working on getting there.

YOU ARE ALL OF MY JOY

I have a serious problem with my body
It has produced both a love and hate that I fluctuate in wanting to
destroy

I woke up today and saw you sleeping
You were soft, gentle
A site of why I should make even more of my life than what I have

When you opened your eyes, I saw it written there
How the world could and would be a better place
If only I could follow the light of your eyes

Your words, "Mommy, I love you," sounded as if I had won the Noble
prize for being the greatest person on earth

Your touch explained that there is a thing called love
That can and will forever exist as long as we have each other

And when you smiled
When you smiled
I knew that I had been given life for a reason...
For however long, or short
It was worth living

But then... then that ugly thought of past experiences
Had to come and mess everything up

In your face I saw myself
Partly, my better self
Staged for the world
Then
I saw the dark night
The face of the unknown
Remembering that for you I had to be violated
Forced to endure the surrender of self control
Then live to tell about it
Have my mind remember that it was not supposed to be this way

Then the real fight began
You were there
Growing inside of me
Demanding attention when I was trying to forget the part of my life
that began your existence

You put everything center stage
Refusing to understand my misery
Until you found a way out

Then you came
Me vowing to want no part of you
Refusing to ever look upon your face...

I was weak
The curiosity of wanting to see that which had controlled my life
trapped me

I remember how it felt to be knocked out by love
I would take you
Care for you
Remembering that you are my good
In no way responsible for my bad experience

But...
today I cannot

Having forgotten about my pledge of never getting tired
Confusing you too often with days filled with laughter and then
Others with cold silence and rejection

So my child,
While I am in a state that thinks only of your best interest
Trying to capture the love before it turns to hate
Please forgive me
Understand that this is why
I am taking my life and giving you yours

This piece takes me to a place of inexplicable grief; touching the most sensitive nerve; using words to tap into un-lived emotions with uncanny precision. If the latter is true of my work, then this piece becomes my best example to demonstrate that writing is a vehicle to connect us to our inner strength, helping each person to heal the world. *Your Are All of My Joy*, connects so many of the dots. It deals with the oppression of women and the violation of our lives through the consistent, repeated, ignored and accepted acts of rape.

In it, I also channel my own feelings of rejection as a child and my insistence that if we love our children fully, they can make us better people. The outcomes I suggest here, with a depressed and mean mother choosing to take her own life instead of terrorizing her child, alludes to how serious and sacred I believe the act of raising a child should be. If you cannot figure out how to do it without seriously injuring the spirit of a child, even if you have been raped, then the person should do whatever it takes not to injure the child.

Victims of rape and the awareness of the pervasiveness of this brutal act in our society became an entrenched part of my consciousness while I was a resident of the Hunter College dormitories, next door to Bellevue Hospital. It started with responding to a call to become a *Rape Crisis Intervention Counselor*. A few evenings a month I would be on call to go next door and be with any woman who was brought in after being raped.

Our primary job as counselors, was to be present for the victim and make sure that the evidence kit, the most crucial and neglected piece of evidence, was appropriately collected and secured. To say that this experience was a humbling does not do it justice. To experience, along with the victim, the total disrespect, disregard and indifference towards women who state they have been violated by a man is indescribable. It sets the stage to understand the psychological power of abuse over any group.

There is no misunderstanding the message to women who are victims of rape, or their supporters. The message I heard then, and continue to hear today is that -- if you do not accept, tolerate and endure the abuse done unto you, your plight will worsen. Every stage of the process that "officially" deals with a woman that states she has been raped, begins and ends with the assumption that every sexual act that involves a female and a male is consensual, with intercourse with her husband being held in the highest regard.

This assumption suggests that we live in a society that has a word -- rape -- for an act it does not believe is possible. For an act of rape to occur, there would need to be true acceptance that females have a right to choose with whom, and when they are sexually active. There is very little in the lived reality of women's lives, or in practiced law that I have observed which supports a woman's right to make decisions regarding her sexuality, or sexual experiences. Anita Hill was and is an extremely intelligent woman that decided to tell the truth about her former boss, a male. We all watched as the United States of America via our elected leaders, mostly male, humiliated her, and by extension, every female in our society.

My impression is that the woman with the most "luck" of successfully prosecuting her rapist is a married woman. If this were to occur, it would not be her virtue that was on trial, but that someone else violated her husband's property. The ignorance of it all seems to suggest that young single females who go out without their boyfriends, or do not have a boyfriend, get what they deserve for being out without a male. Should her date desire sexual intercourse and she does not, and thus is raped by the male she chose to go out with, the tactic silent assumptions are that: the female should have known that this was part of the deal, "had it coming", or that she wanted to have sex, lead the male on and then changed her mind. This dynamic places females in the unjust predicament of accepting rape as a part of their lives and pretending that it did not happen. The penalties, consequences and humiliation of daring to accuse a male of rape have been demonstrated to be worse than living with the pain and denial.

This piece, *You Are All My Joy*, is just one version of the consequences of living with the denial of rape. A child will be left motherless, because of the mother's unprocessed grief. It is my belief that while the cost and consequences of all the unprocessed grief in our world is unmeasurable -- it is infinite -- the monetary loss of the suffering is quite easily more than the total sum of the world's GNP. Too often people who hurt, hurt others, perpetuating pain and suffering. Only when people who hurt seek healing we will ever be able to end the pain and suffering of the world.

DRLONI AIN'T NO NICKNAME

Now get this
Dig it
And get it good

DrLoni ain't no nickname
Taking seven years to reinvent myself
I am new

Will school you
Break it down
Before you have decided I know what I'm talking about

I can code you
Reconstruct you
And quantify your deviant behaviors
Leading to the atrocities of history
In the name of democracy and religious freedom

Don't need you to invite me to your... ta-ta-tahs
Picking my brain
This is insane

I see everything you assume I don't

Reserving courses for white folks assumed more competent
More malleable than me
Having your real conversations in private
Only to publicly ask me it I prefer
Choice A or B

The white male hierarchy must be retained for nostalgia
Doing too good of a job creating expensive copy
Promoting your unwavering commitment to social justice
Not to be real

Step back
Don't touch this

Get out of my way then
Since you decided
In your minimalist assessment of me
What I cannot do

Might as well close your mouth

Astonished -- not by my brilliance
But your misinterpretation of who I am

Didn't just get this way
Always have been me

Ain't gonna change
Ain't got time to beg

Thank you for dis-ing me so soon
My grandmomma ain't raise no fool
Call me by my true names
A constructivist
Embracing culturally relevant pedagogy
Informed by qualitative & quantitative mixed methods
Feminist
Womanist
Art-based interdisciplinary
Dare you to touch this
Forms of inquiry

This ain't no joke

That I've been in
Stay in
The trenches
Ride with privilege
And challenge
Every known construct that tries to define and label me
Trying to squeeze me into one of those tiny little boxes

So get it
Dig it
And get it good
DrLoni ain't no nickname

Given the painful oppression of all women since the beginning of recorded history and black women in American society, please explain why I should conceal my educational accomplishments and reject the use of a term that has been established to honor the achievements of anyone that has achieved as I have?

STARS N' STRIPES

I would love to fly the American flag
My flag
With colors representing
My country
The place I came from
With pride

I mean proud as in
New York City Puerto Rican Proud
The week of the parade
Cruising up 1st and down 2nd
Flags flying on both sides of the ride
Beautiful brown bodies hanging out of every window

Lip smacking sounds ....
"BORICUA MOMMIE", yeah!!!

With the dog's head bobbing in the back
All kinds of hanging shit

Faux fur
Surrounding the Virgin Mother
The red, white and blue
A lone star

I image that maybe I can at least be Jamaican
Having yellow streamers and green cushions with regal lions on the
deck in my well manicured backyard

Everything done with style
No cheap Christmas lights
With bulbs shaped like fruit
Or trees from the tropics

Or maybe it's another flag
From another place
Another country
Draped around the shoulders of my sister
An Olympic star
Carrying the weight of her country
Radiant brown skin reflects the gold

Crying long hard sobs of joy and pride as well
But I can't wear her flag
Any flag

What is my flag?

Is it
Red necks that zoom down a dirt road
I run for my life

YAHOO!!! -- GET NIGRA!!!
YOU DARK B----!!!
They want a piece of me
Strung up
Hung up

The American flag
Streaming proud
With all fifty stars
13 stripes
Along the side of a beat up pickup
Snaps back
Stings me
A drop of blood forms on the side of my mouth
The blood is wiped away

My blood... has so subtly stained
Many an American flag
For my country

This piece is so beautiful in my eyes as it tells of the longing I experienced as a twenty-something year old woman. Along with the perpetual quest to figure out who I was and where I fit in, I wanted something to which I could strongly identify, no longer having a family unit, friends, a boyfriend; just nothing and no one. One Spring I found myself envious of Puerto Rican New Yorkers and the Puerto Rican Day Parade.

The scene I described, a car load of beautiful Puerto Rican males calling to me with love, respect and pure pride actually happened. It was imprinted onto my memory as I vicariously experienced what it felt like again to be deeply connected to something outside of yourself. Then years later, watching Cathy Freeman at the Olympics, I found myself longing to also be able to wear a flag draped around my shoulders, proud... honoring all the ancestors from which I had sprung.

My longing is that we could all live in a world where every person, no matter where they are born, could be proud of and identify with their country of origin. Would it not be wonderful if everyone has an occasion to wear their national flag draped around their shoulders, feeling both the love and the prideful caress of their national fabric?

I CAN'T BELIEVE WHAT SOME FOLKS
DON'T EVEN THINK ABOUT

I can't believe what some folk don't even think about
Take for granted
That the world will always be as it is
Compliant

With white males on top
Not at some point thinking that folks won't
Get tired of seeing his face

Don't you ever wonder what will happen?

Do you think that they are truly satisfied?
And happy???

Watching you eat
Not spitting in your food

Did you think that the chickens really do not
Come home to roost

Even as you silenced Malcolm
Did you not wonder what would happen to the spirit of fire
born in the breast of the young?

Do you think that black women
All women
Would not think
But I wiped your ass?

Do you think the majority,
do not want to take our place?

Mother Africa will be reborn
Thank you, sisters

What do you think the raped and exploited think about you?
Once you are done

Don't you wonder where the anger lies
Where it festers
Waiting to explode
Spurring blood and pus

The women whose children you took were our mothers
Did you not think
In private
We would not learn their stories?
Store the anger?
Come back to get you?

Do you really believe that there is nothing there?
We enjoy it?
It is right?
Your privilege?

And what about the way you exploit your brothers
Regardless of color
Deciding that only a chosen few should share the prize

For some
Now
It is here
Being white is not enough

White angry males will kill us all
Revengeful because they too have been cheated
From what they feel is their entitlement

As people of color break the barriers
The ignorant ones see there is no truth in the stereotypes
We are not lesser
They -- having lived off of being white
Going no where
Lash out at us all
The truth is revealed
RUN FOR COVER AMERICA!!!

Do you not ever wonder what your stepson felt?
All the people that built
America
With the lives of our ancestors
And Guardian Spirits

Did you not even wonder what really sustains them?
Keeps them alive through your exploitation

You felt it was mumblings
Voodoo
Nonsense
Did you really believe that it was you?

How well you have deceived yourself
Not to even question

The Spirits of the Dead
Will raise up
With the Spirits of those who live

Chinese American blood underneath the railroad tracks
Irish American too
The enslaved, all blacks are American soil
Its color comes from our lives

There is only one native son and daughter
Who taught us what this land was
Knew how to co-exist with her
Watch out!!!
The buffalo is an angry spirit

Do you not think that when it wakes
she will not hear the cries of her first child?
Back to the Asian daughter and African man that crossed over
Before the water covered our path

Do you think about where you will be on that day
When Jesus comes?
And you see how much he looks like me?

I can't believe what some folk don't think about
Or if you do
How well you hide your ignorance and the fear of your inevitable
demise.

Learning how to release my judgment of other's intellectual capacity and their apparent inability to think critically, is an area in which I am constantly striving to grow. The title of this piece is the refrain that pops into my head when I engage with other human beings in the world. When a white person steps in front of me while in line, cuts me off when I am speaking, publicly attempts to "check me"... puts me down, or when a young male student, not even twenty years of age uses profanity towards me, in a university classroom... in front of other students... I am amazed! The other white people observing the incident and the one projecting the action state that they "do not get it." While these white people self-profess that they do not understand; are "absolutely clueless," to use the term they have used with me, they are always equally certain that the disrespect I have experienced is not related to race or gender. It is in these situations that I struggle with the cognitive dissonance between what has occurred and what I perceive as the other person's intellectual capacity, and now by extension, their lack of integrity.

In these incidents I do not believe for a moment that they, "do not get it"," but blatantly reject that their actions are part of the systemic practice of racism that still vigorously exists. If I become angry in these situations, it is not because a white person has observed my daily dose of racism in America, and yet again said nothing; it is because they insult my intelligence as they attempt to redefine my experience and perceptions to feed their state of ignorance and denial.

This piece echoes the first chapter in this book; End White Silence. Feigning ignorance and choosing denial, while pretending not to see, is what nurtures racism. Anyone that is able to act in a manner which perpetuates racism, is also intelligent enough to stop it. Thus, I am stuck with my perpetual amazement and judgment of what others seemingly appear not to think about.

SOFT BY NATURE
HARD WITHOUT A CHOICE

My stuff is soft because I don't let it get too hard

If I let it get too hard, then the muscles on the side of my head
tighten and I begin to think
concentrate
get angry and dangerously analyze -- then question

I start to ask questions like
why are children starving and the country in which I live, work and
thrive as a creative person
helping to better the world
supporting the soldiers that starve them?

I want to know why my country is trying to decide how your
country should be run and why I feel an alliance with you and not
my country?

Tell me Mr. President
You lie, and I have to believe you when you said that you didn't, but
then admit that you did

Tell me, why you overlook me and suppress my sisters and brothers

Tell me, huh... someone tell me

Why am I here?
What is my role?
Where is my home?

You see, the stuff is getting hard and the sides of my head are beginning to hurt

I am soft by nature, but hard without a choice

Even at the ripe age of forty-six, now forty-eight, I struggle with the dishonesty of the politicians that control so much of society and our indifference to the corruption that exists. The state of perpetually being baffled by the indifference and ignorance that pervades our society overshadows my professional practice and is evident in all my creative output.

On one hand I think, "I should know better" or "not get upset," but I am glad that I have resisted the cliches of indifference and laziness that have overtaken too many members of our society. Although, having rarely observed otherwise, I refuse to accept that a tolerance for corruption and a lack of integrity are requisite characteristics for all individuals that hold positions of authority. I still expect and want to follow leaders that are above board, intelligent, fair, and rational individuals with a heightened sense of moral character. My professional life has been a blend between the search to find, or become, that which I seek.

SKIN-TONE

After sitting and watching "Ethnic Notions" I asked more thoughtful
questions
What were my emotions about skin tone

Some of this seems so unnecessary,
since
I didn't know that Grandma was high yellow... it seems,
until after I went to college

That's also when I discovered I was a produce of a single parent
household,
Or something called an extended family

I just thought it was normal

"Ethnic Notions" made me question if I had my own hangups
Is that what this "black stuff" is supposed to do?
Cast doubt where there is none?

Is my thinking I had no doubts just another form of a hangup?

Is thinking I may have a preference towards darker men some sort
of rejection of my lighter brothers and sisters?
Do I really like lighter men, but say that I prefer them darker
because I think it's the correct choice?
Do I really have a preference?

But Grandma was light?

My heart does race faster when I see a tall dark skin brother,
Our heart won't go along with any lie that the mind creates
Or will it?

But then the only man
Young man at the time, that I ever loved was light, most would say
yellow
That wasn't an issue unless we were admiring how good our skin
looked and felt next to each other

I hope he didn't love me because I was darker than he was?

We were going to name our first daughter Ebony Sunshine, without
thinking what color she was going to be

I wonder if he, as he has grown older, has thought about that?

I'm more confused about color
Its interpretation and meaning
Didn't know it had meaning in the black community until I got to
be an adult

Just knew that I loved Grandma and that I was her girl
Never knew that it could have been possible for her to love me more
or less because of it

I miss my Grandma

A good bit of this book has fleshed out as my continued mourning and missing of my grandparents... especially my grandmother. It seems that so much of what I have to say and my beliefs return back to them and the way they raised me. The beauty of what my grandparents did, was that they just simply always did the right thing, and if they did not, or could not do something as expected, they just said so. Life does not have to be as complicated as so many of us make it, or in my case, as I have allowed it to be, tolerating unhealthy relationships in my world.

The predominance and pre-occupation with skin-tone, and the "good-hair, bad-hair" dichotomy is one of the most unhealthily manifestations of low self-esteem within the black community. Fortunately, it has alluded me most of my life.

Within our home the skin color of other blacks was just something that was never talked about. Within our immediate family we were across the spectrum. Grandma was the lightest with beautiful white golden silver gray hair and green, then gray, then hazel eyes that changed with her moods. As a child I stared into her eyes, then my own, trying to figure out if all eyes changed colors, or if it was just something that was special about her. To this day I have not met, or been in a relationship close enough with anyone to experience seeing three different eye colors. Even with my grandmother having three different eye colors, and a light complexion, I cannot think of an extended discussion on the topic that hinted at this being something that made her better or more special.

In my world my grandmother was the beginning and the end. That status had nothing to do with her being fair skinned with light eyes, but primarily because she just was. Every action that took place within our home had to meet her approval. The foundation for my grandmother's all consuming authority was that things always turned out exactly how my grandmother predicted, and if not, she could always find a way to make things better. Just being near her or my grandfather made me feel loved and safe. I knew from experience that if either of them were around, no one would say mean things to me, while that omnipresent physical ache of loneliness and hurt disappeared whenever I was near them.

As a little girl, I clearly remember being fascinated by my grand-mother's changing color eyes. During those ubiquitous moments of crafting together, often touching arm to arm, or me just finding a reason to lean into, or lay on her, I would always look through the top of her glasses, above the bifocal and into her eyes. Her eyes would be most visible and illuminated for me within the light of the sewing machine that separated our faces. I would look up at her past the light and into her eyes as I fulfilled my duty of threading the sewing machine needle. As I did this she would gaze out over her glasses offering me a clear and unobstructed view of her eyes. Once I decided to seize the moment and asked,

"Grandma, what color are your eyes?" and her reply,

"Baby, Grandma doesn't know;" which to me always translated to, then it is not all that important. If there was anything that mattered to me and in my world, my grandparents always knew about it. If they did not, well... I guess I figured it was not that important, because Grandma knew everything!

My younger cousin was the darkest with a smooth dark chocolatey complexion; the first chocolate drop with whom I feel in love. As the older cousin, if only by a few years, I would force him to play school, giving him so much homework and holding "school" for so long that he entered kindergarten knowing how to read, write and do math. His kindergarten ceremony, they did not do ridiculous graduations back then, which I attended with his mother, was an exciting day for me. I can still see his picture in his golden gown against his chocolate complexion with those full smooth cheeks. I loved his skin so much, thinking his complexion was a more "real brown" than mine, like the brown in the crayon box. I could not resist myself and would grab him so I could kiss his cheeks and squeeze their plumpness, taking bites with my lip covered teeth. Being a typical little boy, he would of course resist and scream. We ended up rolling on the floor tussling, with him yelling, yet laughing, for me to stop. I was still stronger, so I could still pin him pretty good. If he yelled loud enough my grandmother would eventually begin to fuss at us to stop; saying she didn't have time to take anyone's child to the hospital.

In between my grandmother and cousin, we were a collection of caramel and chocolates, but none better, or worse than the other. It seems that once there was a hushed conversation with an aunt, my grandmother's sister, who was even lighter than my grandmother. I was looking at a picture of my grandmother as a younger woman that to me was almost unrecognizable and loudly exclaimed,

"But...she looks so white!"

I was told that she had a hard time as a young girl because of her complexion, and then, her really red hair. Immediately, I had an attack of retro anger at anyone that would ever make fun of my grandmother, or make her feel bad, for any reason.

In my child's head, I began to struggle with the concept of how or why, my grandmother was teased about being "light enough to pass," but that there were some people that acted as if they, or others were better if they were light and could pass. At that time I knew nothing of context. The deep south of Mississippi in the earlier 1900s was a different place than the 50s and 60s of New York City, where with age my grandmother's complexion became more rich and tanned and her hair color turned that beautiful blonde silver gray. So, I guess that in some ways this absence of skin-tone being an issue or topic in our home, was because it had already been such an issue in my grandmother's life.

This poem ends on the still most important note for me, I miss my grandma.

WEEDS

I've lived too long and have seen too much to ever believe in rain-
bows again

Too many of my sunny days have been rained on
Too many ideal situation gone bad

I've watched winners lose and people of standards succumb for a
cheap price

I know -- that when love and beauty grow -- it flourishes
leaving room for nothing more
but sometimes
without notice
weeds do seep in

My course of action is to find a situation and,
keep it weedless for as long as I possibly can

When the weeds begin to sprout,
I simply pick up and plant my garden elsewhere

Knowing that I wrote this before my twenty-first birthday and seeing that I embraced a dichotomous sense of power over the JOY and misery in my life makes me both sad and angry. Sad, because too many children and young adults are put in the position of having to negotiate having love in their lives, and angry because often the very people that are granted responsibility to help a child in a negative situation, sometimes only make it worst.

As a society and educational community we have failed the majority of children born to parents that do not "act like" they love their children. Instead of truly helping children, we lean towards enabling incompetent parents and looking the other way. Many have questioned,

"Why is it that you need a license to have a dog, or drive a car, but anyone can have a child?"

This piece reflects the response of an adolescent coming into adulthood having to negotiate difficult situations with limited support. No child, nor the wounded adult they become, should have to deal with a life of loss, isolation and abandonment, because they are only given the choice of conditional love, the garden, in exchange for tolerating abuse, the weeds.

The undertone of my professional life has been the expectation that there should be a system of accountability which requires parents to be responsible for their children's well-being. My life's work will be complete only when America has options of quality schooling for all children. No one should be able to bring a life into this world without demonstrating the ability to love and nurture their child, society's most sacred and precious gift.

THE MAGIC OF FORTY

40 years of searching for love, with so little success
I finally decide to love myself
Love me, myself and I as we sassy high schoolers said
Being flip
Not knowing so much
Yet knowing everything
I begin to search
Re-discover
At 25
After the first broken heart
Not enough money
Years of not being skinny
Bad relationships
Unkind friends
The ones that gossip about you
Then act like it's funny when you over hear their mean comments
What happens to the girls that can't laugh it off?
Outcast

Loners
Alone
No sisters
No brothers
No real best friends
There no matter what
Trying to fit into someone else's family after your own begins to wear
away
No more chicken with Aunt Grace & Gloria
No more Grandma and Grandpa
The end

The beginning...
Tired of being tired
Still no one to love you back... for real
No escape
You have to stay here
Make it to forty
Being one of those incredible women you read so much about
They wear purple
Are not concerned about their weight
And wear uncoordinated shoes

I promise myself to keep it together
Do what brings me JOY
Not sure why I have to wait for forty
But knowing that it will be my time

Then it begins to creep up at 35
I begin to see the bottom of the hill as I slide to 40
Then see the sun go up at 39
I plot and plan a wonderful future

It's an uneventful day
Others are mad at me for something
This is now the norm
Now that I am okay
Anger is the only retaliation against me

But I really don't give a ...
Yes, I've arrived

I put on a "few extra pounds"
But I love my body,
Well some parts
But the magic is that I accept it all

There is still no one to love me
So I have to do it myself
It's good
Not complete
I release my "good" job to play with paint
I am happy
Keep my beautiful home

Life is good after forty

The climb to get to this place of forty-six, then forty-seven, now forty-eight, has been pretty amazing. Just this morning preparing to write, I realized that the forties are just the prep work for the absolutely fabulous fifties! I can feel it and know without asking that this will be my reality. I am also a bit giddy with excitement thinking about the loving experiences, career shift, new professional encounters and the... hold onto my seat, because I now know and accept that I am worthy of love, WTW (Worth-The-Wait) man that will enter my life!

An interesting observation I made during my forties is what happens as I listen to the rhythms of my body and incorporate physical activity into my days. The first frustrating, yet happy reality, is that I really do not need, or want, to eat as much as I use to. The more I listen and eat as my body desires, the more lean I become and the better I feel. When I add exercise to this mix, I am back to having more males speak to me on the streets, and feeling that sense of confidence that naturally makes you hold your head higher.

Now understand me, males speaking to me on the streets is not the goal or desire, but it has been a very reliable indicator of good physical fitness and appearance for the majority of my life. No matter how we slice it, we are mammals with animal instincts. My journey is to find the healthy balance of being at peace with the attention I receive because of my appearance, and not shaping who or what I am in an attempt to control or lessen that attention.

Too much of my life has been spent down playing my physical appearance, because of the jealousy of other females and not knowing how to deal with inappropriate and disrespectful male attention as a young woman. The other females in my life seemed to be more accepting of me "when I didn't look so good." In my ignorance, I constantly toed the line of dressing and wearing my hair, to allow other females to feel better about being around me and hopefully win their affection. The crazy part is that I am still consistently shunned by insecure females and not invited to anything where I might shine too brightly.

When it came to dealing with males, as an attractive young woman, I decided that it was safer not to attract too much attention, so I could be left alone. After years of my grandmother "pulling my hair out" with the hot comb at the kitchen stove, I wore my... "below the shoulder, not a weave, black girl hair," up in bun from adolescence to my mid-twenties. It was amazing to observe that the same guys who ignored me one day, would speak and... said in perfect high school vernacular...

"Be all up in my face," the next day if I wore my hair down. When I finally found the confidence to wear my long hair out, the ridicule I experienced as a result of it, eventually lead me to return to styles which concealed my length and then to eventually cut it all off. The insanely funny part of my hair journey, to shun the jealousy and attention of having long hair, was that I received even more attention, from both men and women, with my new and unintentional short and sexy look!

Laughing, I confess that I am probably... "loc'd for life." My hair, now loc'd, is back to being long and fiercely resists every and any attempt for me to conceal its beauty. My short hair, and now my longer locs have been liberating. Hair, like children can be amazing teachers if we allow it.

So, the great news, after having done my 30s and so far most of my 40s alone, with no consistent life sustaining love with which I could identify, is recognizing that I need not wait for fifty to get it right. The permission I have been seeking to have a fantastic life is the gift I gave myself for my forty-seventh birthday.

The Magic of Forty is also liberating because it does a poor job of relating all the very sad ups and downs of my life before and after forty. Doing a poor job of relating this reality is a good thing, because it signals that I have truly begun to let go of that which needs to be gone from my world. Life is too precious and short, to dwell on, or give attention to the nonsense that I have released. I need not relate line and verse the who done what and how, because it truly is not worth my time. The time that I have allowed negative people and situation to take from me is all they get, no need to engage in a replay.

Watch out world, I am ready to fully accept my bountiful blessings; "Hello to my wonderful life!"

A CALL TO ACTION

AMADOU AMADOU AMADOU AMADOU AMADOU AMADOU
AMADOU AMADOU AMADOU AMADOU
DAILLO

AMADOU AMADOU AMADOU AMADOU AMADOU AMADOU
AMADOU AMADOU AMADOU AMADOU

Can you hear, or do you still want to believe
It's a tragedy

The tragedy is our own deafness -- the
"This is awful"
"This should not happen"

It happens because we LET it happen

We don't show up
Turn out

Protest
March
Vote certain folks out of office when we need to

It happens because we don't do enough of what we should
SACRIFICE
Until it's over
Until we are there

It's a mother getting up at 4 am, after bed at 1 am
Taking children to the sitter "near my sister's house, in that better
school district"
Then the A train
Back to the hood
Then the jungle, to work a nine to five
To go back to school
To go back home
All before the MetroCard

It's - NO - you can't have those sneakers
Those clothes
Anything you believe will get you "the look"
Oh! now because it's supporting a black man
"This is us?"
NOT US - all our skin folk ain't always our kin folk, she said
But them
Getting over on you
Making $$$$$ off your low self-esteem

Capitalism - is truly American
Democracy
We don't discriminate... but will exploit all equally

When I finally get mine, I forget you are my brother
Brother

Look at me leapin n' jumpin n' hoppin for the man
Singing the song they tell me to

-- and us --

Caring about showing up to a movie on the first night
So what???
We can show we know how to go to the MOVIES!!!

It's letting ourselves hear -- and feel -- what we need to
And then doing it

Showing up at school so they know, somebody gives a damn
So if the overcrowded, don't give ah... about our kids, not caring
schools
Because we LET them
Decide to put your child in the back of the room, and time out
Everyday
All day
They will think twice,
because somebody gives a damn!

Especially his momma...
Who shows up,
drunk & high
Tells the principal what he can do with himself
Addresses the teacher as "Ms. B,"
and her conversation
"Don't be dissin my child, he here to learn, and I spec you to teach!"

She leaves
Amidst chuckles and looks of teachers too distraught to speak

A classmate laughs at Nymel
About to say a your momma line
Nymel
PROUD
Knowing he is loved
No matter how messed up it is
Responds

"FORGET YOU PUNK!!!
My momma was here!"

He
Never to spend another whole day in time out
Because he knows when his is bored
Entitled to every bit of this mis-education

And when you don't have enough sense to show up
It's wrapping your arms around your 2 yr old
8 yr old,
18 yr old and saying

I LOVE YOU
.... and meaning it

Holding them until you are both uncomfortable
So long that it no longer feels uncomfortable
But it feels good...
Damn good!

Not like the

it feel good, then it don't of an orgasm that was never had
cept' that once
him takin' long enough so she had a chance to come
and then collapsing on top of her
too tired to move
heavy

She pretending....
Liking the warmth of him being there
Not having to -- quick fast -- jump up and get back to
"acting" like a man
Whatever that is

Not being able to feel for as long as you wanted, because you're
afraid of being soft???

Mothers & Fathers
Sisters & Brothers
Whatever
It's holding your children -- our children,
Holding ourselves
Long enough and strong enough
So we know what love feels like
Not caught up in an endless un-ful-filling cycle of sexual behavior

AMADOU AMADOU AMADOU AMADOU

I'm sorry for all the times I was not there
I supported the system with my silence

Fake negroes, with remarks about being on the plantation come
Monday morning
So, if it's all that

And you ain't a house negro
Why you show up???

And not Saturday a.m.
After they shot our grandmother down in her apartment doorway

Drugggggggggg a brother on the back of a truck
Like "just got married" soup cans

A MAN with a stick up his ...???

AMADOU AMADOU AMADOU AMADOU

I hear you brother
Messenger from the Motherland
Yes -- it's time

There is no more motivation -- only action

AMADOU AMADOU AMADOU AMADOU

The tragedy is our inaction
Letting it happen
Instead of snappin'

AMADOU AMADOU AMADOU AMADOU

Hear the call to action
A - MA - DOU, what I got to do

Show up
Manage your business

If you don't
I don't have time for your BS
I can't believe this conversation

It happens because we LET it happen
The only tragedy will be your own inaction
PEACE

There are several pieces in my repertoire which bring me to tears, and for which I have nothing else to say when I am done. This is one of those pieces and the end of this book.

May God's grace and love continue to surround you on this journey called life. And so it is.

FINAL WORD

Thank you for joining me here for the sake of my sanity. Some of you might still want to ask me "how" to do X...Y...Z... or want a simple 1...2... 3... solution to solving all that ails us. I do not have an answer for you; but I will offer you my final word, said as much for myself, as for all that may ask.

Follow the light of whatever allows you to fully love yourself first... and then others. Give as little time as possible to negative people, or to those who have low self-esteem. The lower the ratio of negative people in your world, the higher your JOY factor will be... it is really that simple. Remember... love is always the answer. When loves does not work, apply more love.

WHAT'S NEXT

DrLoni.com - Home base for all things DrLoni.

HmHmC.com - A learning community of families committed to academic excellence for their children.

FortheSakeofMySanity.com - One woman's journey of speaking truth to power and ignorance.

SistersReadingSisters.com - A sisterhood of women that READ, WRITE and ACT to change their lives and the lives of others

Love & light,
Abundant blessings,
DrLoni

ABOUT THE AUTHOR

DrLoni is a native of NYC splitting her time between Milwaukee, Wisconsin and Brooklyn, New York. She began writing as a child and has never stopped. After three decades of working in education, starting as a classroom teacher and ending as a university professor, deciding to write full-time is the single most courageous act of her professional career. Her writing is representational of her life and interests. It is as varied as the prose of the political commentary in her first eBook:

For the Sake of My Sanity: One Women's Journey of
Speaking Truth to Power and Ignorance

to the playfulness of her forth coming books, a cookbook:

Say My Name: A Soul Food Cookbook

and to her life's passion embodied in:

5+5=10: An Equation for Academic Success

She works very hard at her craft to cover up the fact that writing full-time is an elaborate ploy to allow more time for gardening. You can connect with her at:

DrLoni.com
and follow her:
@DrLoni

www.ingramcontent.com/pod-product-compliance
Lightning Source LLC
Chambersburg PA
CBHW060503280326
41933CB00014B/2843